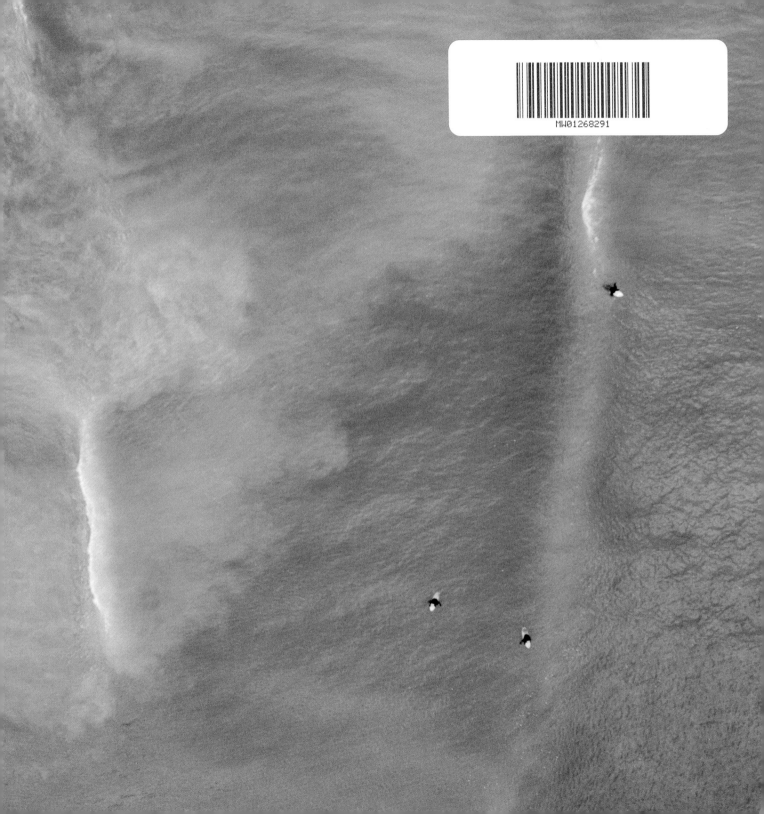

MW01268291

Protecting Our Shoreline.

The Great Lakes region offers some of the most diverse and wondrous resources right at our doorstep. When we step outside, whether to surf in sub-temps or simply go on a walk, we become part of a process that not only effects the future of our outdoor explorations but directly impacts how future generations will experience the same places and activities.

Simply put, our adventures, whatever they may be, must start with protecting our natural assets. As part of our commitment to you, we continue to push the boundaries of potential ways to safeguard our freshwater playground. We recognize the importance of preserving nature's gifts and integrate it into the very core of our business. In fact, we believe M22 only exists because we embody the very essence of the Great Lakes region.

Part of our mission is to vigilantly monitor our operations to ensure the company's environmental footprint is as small as it can be and its environmental contribution is as great as it can be. As we always have and always will, one percent of everything we sell is donated to Leelanau Conservancy and together, with your support, we have contributed more than $100,000 to the preservation and protection of the land and water we all cherish.

M22 also takes pride in collaborating with other companies that share this objective. We partner with The National Parks Service for our annual M22 Challenge, work with FLOW (For Love of Water) to defend our freshwater paradise, and have joined the Great Lakes Business Network to help expose threats to our Great Lakes.

So, as you embark on your next adventure, remember to protect as you explore. Pick up trash on the side of the trail, take out whatever you brought in, volunteer for a local conservation program, or score your favorite piece of M22 gear, and feel proud knowing you're lending a hand and contributing to a greater good.

Micro-adventures.

01 02 03 04 05 06 07 08 09 10 11 12 13 14 15 16 17 18 19 20 21 22 23 24 25 26 27 28 29 30

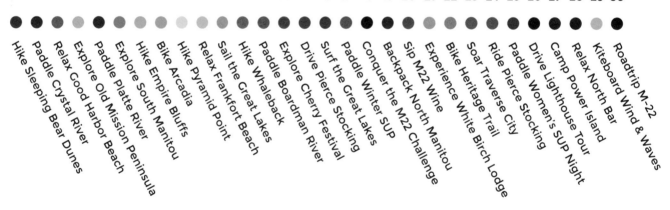

01 Hike Sleeping Bear Dunes
02 Paddle Crystal River
03 Relax Good Harbor Beach
04 Explore Old Mission Peninsula
05 Paddle Platte River
06 Explore South Manitou
07 Hike Empire Bluffs
08 Bike Arcadia
09 Hike Pyramid Point
10 Relax Frankfort Beach
11 Sail the Great Lakes
12 Hike Whaleback
13 Paddle Boardman River
14 Explore Cherry Festival
15 Drive Pierce Stocking
16 Surf the Great Lakes
17 Paddle Winter SUP
18 Conquer the M22 Challenge
19 Backpack North Manitou
20 Sip M22 Wine
21 Experience White Birch Lodge
22 Bike Heritage Trail
23 Soar Traverse City
24 Ride Pierce City
25 Paddle Women's Stocking
26 Drive Lighthouse Tour
27 Camp Women's SUP Night
28 Relax Power Island
29 Kiteboard North Bar
30 Roadtrip Wind & Waves M-22

Life is short. Every day should be an adventure, and it can be—if you make it. Even small moments can be made into something amazing. Life, fun, discovery—it doesn't have to be difficult. The only limit to making a moment worthwhile is yourself and your imagination. Choose a Microadventure and enter the coordinates in your phone to begin. Don't forget to share your Microadventure with us! **@M22LIFE #M22LIFE**

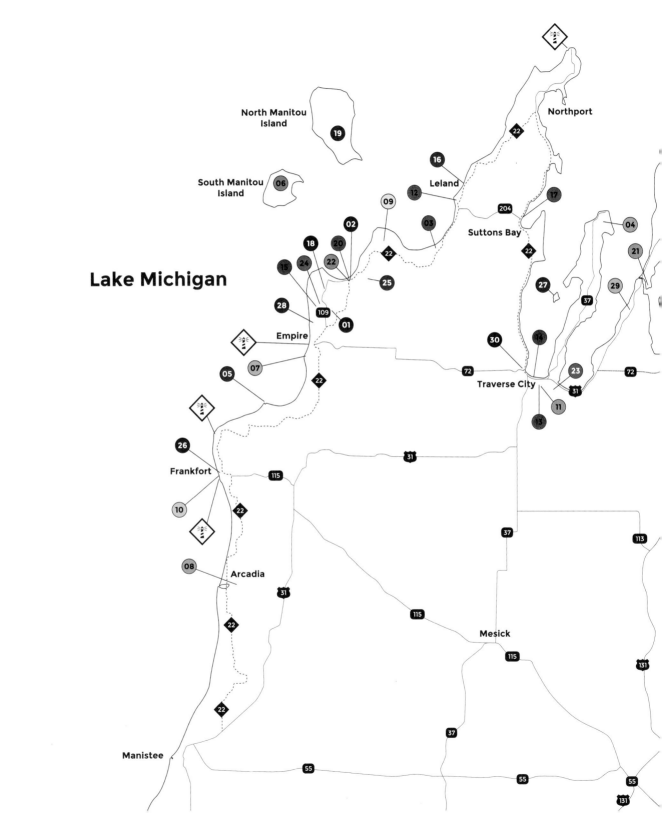

① **Beginner:** Little effort, kid-friendly, accessible.
● **Intermediate:** Some effort, moderate to strenuous activity.
③ **Advanced:** Strenuous activity and/or some risk involved.

① **Short:** 2 hours or less.
● **Medium:** Up to 1/2 day.
③ **Long:** Full day or more; plan ahead.

○ **Wheelchair**   ● **Parking on/near site**
○ **Pets Allowed**   ● **Kid Friendly**

Notes:

Hike

Difficulty ● ● ● ○ ○
Time ● ● ● ○ ○ ○

Sleeping Bear Dunes

Enter coordinates in phone to begin:
44.882672, -86.041601

Take in the Sleeping Bear Dunes like most have never seen them before—from the flip side. Hike over the dune climb while taking in a view of the Manitou Islands, and simply follow the shore north. You'll find some superb views along the way, and hopefully Glen Haven...eventually.

Try to coordinate this adventure with a friend. Drop a vehicle in Glen Haven and carpool to the Dune Climb parking lot. Begin your 7-mile trek from there and end at your parked vehicle for a short cruise back to the Dune Climb. Take a dip in Little Glen across M-109 at the Little Glen Beach Park.

WHAT TO BRING: Plenty of drinking water, sunscreen, snacks, and shoes.

OPTIONAL SIDE TREK: The historic village of Glen Haven is a destination for history buffs, including blacksmith demonstrations. The beach and water colors can't be beat in Glen Haven.

KICK IT UP A NOTCH: Drop off some bikes in Glen Haven before you go, and ride the Sleeping Bear Heritage Trail back to your car to experience one of the best stretches of biking trail in the area.

TIPS: Bring shoes! Sand will get hot and many areas of the beach are covered in rocks. Make sure you get your Sleeping Bear Dunes National Park Pass ahead of time. Stock up on food, as the nearest restaurants or convenience stores are a couple miles away. Afterwards, be sure to stop by Art's Tavern in downtown Glen Arbor for a well-deserved drink after the trek. Bring cash along with you, as they don't accept credit cards.

① **Beginner:** Little effort, kid-friendly, accessible.
● **Intermediate:** Some effort, moderate to strenuous activity.
③ **Advanced:** Strenuous activity and/or some risk involved.

① **Short:** 2 hours or less.
● **Medium:** Up to 1/2 day.
③ **Long:** Full day or more; plan ahead.

○ **Wheelchair**   ● **Parking on/near site**
○ **Pets Allowed**   ● **Kid Friendly**

Notes:

Paddle

Crystal River

Difficulty ● ● ● ○ ○
Time ● ● ● ○ ○

Enter coordinates in phone to begin:

44.897947, -85.983942

Take the family on a 2-3 hour trip along one of northern Michigan's best river rides. With clear, shallow water and a sandy bottom, all tucked deep in the Sleeping Bear Dunes, you'll see why the Crystal River has earned its name.

If you want to paddle your own kayak or SUP, park at Crystal River Outfitters and they will shuttle you 2 miles to the head of the river (675 and Fisher Road) for $10. They take care of it all and will load and unload your equipment. When you arrive back in downtown Glen Arbor be sure to check out our beautiful M22 store and enjoy some wine tasting.

WHAT TO BRING: A cooler for drinks, water shoes with straps (flip-flops may get lost), sunscreen, and a way to secure items like keys and phones in case you go under (like the M22 waterproof bag).

OPTIONAL SIDE TREK: Glen Arbor is full of great shopping, arts, and eats. If that's not enough, rent some bikes at Crystal River Outfitters and head down the Sleeping Bear Heritage Trail for a gorgeous view of the scenery.

KICK IT UP A NOTCH: Opt for a SUP (stand up paddle). It's surprisingly stable and easy to do and gives you a different perspective (and workout).

TIPS: Just have fun. You really can't go wrong with this trip, even if you tip!

- **Beginner:** Little effort, kid-friendly, accessible.
- ② **Intermediate:** Some effort, moderate to strenuous activity.
- ③ **Advanced:** Strenuous activity and/or some risk involved.

- ① **Short:** 2 hours or less.
- **Medium:** Up to 1/2 day.
- ③ **Long:** Full day or more; plan ahead.

- ○ **Wheelchair**
- **Pets Allowed**
- **Parking on/near site**
- **Kid Friendly**

Notes:

Relax

Difficulty ● ○ ○ ○ ○ ○
Time ● ● ● ○ ○ ○

Good Harbor Beach

Enter coordinates in phone to begin:
44.947390, -85.811444

Good Harbor Beach: the perfect place to reconnect with friends and nature. It's secluded yet accessible, and one of the best beaches in northern Michigan. Set aside an evening to enjoy a sunset around a bonfire, and maybe catch a shooting star or two!

WHAT TO BRING: Drinking water and/or other beverages, just no glass. Food and picnic items (s'mores!) are always a good idea, as well as firewood, blankets, swim gear and a camera.

OPTIONAL SIDE TREK: Good Harbor beach is only 15 minutes from Pyramid Point; it might be worthwhile to check out both in one day.

KICK IT UP A NOTCH: From either Bohemia Beach or anywhere along Good Harbor Beach, take a walk to the west and discover the amazing river mouth of Shalda Creek. You can also drive there by heading west on Lake Michigan Road. This spot is not to be missed.

TIPS: If you pick a spot a bit off the beaten path, you'll have what seems like the whole beach to yourself. Also, remember to take care of your fire properly! Dig a pit into the sand to create your firepit, and put water on it after you're done. A common mistake people make is to bury the fire in the sand. However, this can mean you're simply insulating hot coals for anyone to accidentally step on—possibly children. Please keep the beach clean so everyone can enjoy.

● **Beginner:** Little effort, kid-friendly, accessible.
② **Intermediate:** Some effort, moderate to strenuous activity.
③ **Advanced:** Strenuous activity and/or some risk involved.

① **Short:** 2 hours or less.
● **Medium:** Up to 1/2 day.
③ **Long:** Full day or more; plan ahead.

● **Wheelchair** ● **Parking on/near site**
● **Pets Allowed** ● **Kid Friendly**

Notes:

Explore

Old Mission Peninsula

Difficulty ● ○ ○ ○ ○ ○
Time ● ● ● ○ ○ ○

Enter coordinates in phone to begin:

44.989949, -85.479675

Old Mission Peninsula is the perfect place to unwind after a hectic week. Nestled in the middle of Grand Traverse Bay, OMP is still close to town, but far enough away for almost any summer activity imaginable.

WHAT TO BRING: Camera, swimming gear, and possibly some spending money for some of the area's best wineries.

OPTIONAL SIDE TREK: Old Mission offers some of the most scenic road riding in the area. Bring your road bike and cruise the loop along the edge of the peninsula. Follow the east side north, all the way to the lighthouse. Once there, ride back to town along the west shoreline. Alternatively, take a dip at Haserot Beach. Bring your mask and snorkel to look for some underwater wrecks right off the beach.

KICK IT UP A NOTCH: Bring a SUP or kayak on a calm day and head on out to Power Island, an island nestled in the heart of West Grand Traverse Bay. Launch from Bowers Harbor boat launch; it's about a 3-mile paddle to the island. There are miles of hiking trails out at the Old Mission Lighthouse. Park at the Lighthouse and review the trail map. You can either hike some of the short inner loops or spend some more time and hike the outer loop. This area is also great for trail running.

TIPS: While OMP is famous for its wineries, there are also plenty of great hidden spots to grab a snack or a more formal bite to eat. Among our favorites are Jolly Pumpkin Restaurant & Brewery and the Old Mission General Store.

05

① **Beginner:** Little effort, kid-friendly, accessible.
● **Intermediate:** Some effort, moderate to strenuous activity.
③ **Advanced:** Strenuous activity and/or some risk involved.

① **Short:** 2 hours or less.
● **Medium:** Up to 1/2 day.
③ **Long:** Full day or more; plan ahead.

○ **Wheelchair**   ● **Parking on/near site**
○ **Pets Allowed**   ● **Kid Friendly**

Notes:

Paddle

Difficulty ● ● ● ○ ○
Time ● ● ● ○ ○

Platte River

Enter coordinates in phone to begin:
44.711037, -86.118796

The Platte River is split up into two sections; the Upper and Lower Platte. The Lower Platte trip is the most popular and user-friendly. There are parking lots, public restrooms, and launches at the beginning and end of Lake Michigan road. We suggest dropping a bike off at Platte River point and parking and launching up near M-22. This trip takes around two hours and is absolutely beautiful. The river is slow, shallow and family friendly. The park at the end of the trip is one of our favorite places in all of Michigan and a great place to picnic and make some memories with the family.

The Upper Platte section is a fast-paced, spring-fed river that has a quick current and average depth of 2-3 feet. There are low-hanging branches and underwater obstacles making it geared more toward the experienced paddler. On this 4-hour-trip you are more than likely to tip so be prepared to get wet.

WHAT TO BRING: A cooler for drinks (no glass please), water shoes with straps (flip-flops might get lost), sunscreen, and a way to secure items like keys and phones in case you go under (like the M22 waterproof bag). Be sure to bring cash or credit if you are renting a vessel for this trip.

OPTIONAL SIDE TREK: Want to turn back time a bit? Swing by The Cherry Bowl Drive-in Theatre for a one-of-a-kind northern Michigan experience to finish out your day.

TIPS: Both the Honor Trading Post and Riverside Canoe Trips offer kayaks, canoes or stand up paddles for rent on the Platte River. A Sleeping Bear Dunes National Park Pass is required for Lower Platte trips.

06

- ① **Beginner:** Little effort, kid-friendly, accessible.
- ● **Intermediate:** Some effort, moderate to strenuous activity.
- ③ **Advanced:** Strenuous activity and/or some risk involved.

- ① **Short:** 2 hours or less.
- ② **Medium:** Up to 1/2 day.
- ● **Long:** Full day or more; plan ahead.

- ○ Wheelchair
- ○ Pets Allowed
- ● Parking on/near site
- ● Kid Friendly

Notes:

Explore

South Manitou

Difficulty ● ● ● ○ ○
Time ● ● ● ● ● ●

Enter coordinates in phone to begin:
45.010386, -86.094811

Grab a pack, climb aboard a historic ferry, and get ready to party like it's 1834. This day trip takes you through a historic ghost town, an ancient cedar forest, near a shipwreck, and around some of the most beautiful and secluded beaches in northern Michigan.

WHEN TO GO: Catch the early morning boat to allow plenty of time for fun on the island. Buy your tickets and get the schedule at **manitoutransit.com** (be sure to reserve in advance).

WHAT TO BRING: Drinking water and/or a filtration system, food, comfortable daypack, camera, good hiking shoes, swimsuits, and hammocks.

OPTIONAL SIDE TREK: Arrive in Leland early and take a walk around Historic Fishtown, where you'll find a smattering of quaint shops and old shanties—a booming place for fishermen back in the day.

TIPS: Be sure to book your reservation in advance; the boat fills up fast on weekends and popular holidays. You'll need a park pass, but don't worry—you can get everything you need at the ferry station that morning. Just plan an extra 20 minutes for parking and permits. Pack an extra day's worth of food! At least a few times a year, the ferry has to suspend its service due to weather (think 10-foot swells) and leave the islanders stranded. Its happened twice to our field researcher, and she's never regretted being prepared.

① **Beginner:** Little effort, kid-friendly, accessible.
● **Intermediate:** Some effort, moderate to strenuous activity.
③ **Advanced:** Strenuous activity and/or some risk involved.

● **Short:** 2 hours or less.
② **Medium:** Up to 1/2 day.
③ **Long:** Full day or more; plan ahead.

○ **Wheelchair**
○ **Pets Allowed**
● **Parking on/near site**
● **Kid Friendly**

07

Notes:

Hike

Empire Bluffs

Difficulty ● ● ● ○ ○
Time ● ● ○ ○ ○ ○

Enter coordinates in phone to begin:

44.799404, -86.058626

Explore one of Michigan's most scenic natural overlooks. Perched hundreds of feet above Lake Michigan, Empire Bluff Trail offers spectacular views of the surrounding area year-round and is easily accessible.

WHAT TO BRING: You won't need much besides some good shoes and a camera! The hike is 1.5 miles round trip and fairly hilly, so water is never a bad idea.

OPTIONAL SIDE TREK: When the boardwalk ends, take the trail that continues on along the bluff to the south. Tread carefully. You will be rewarded with more spectacular views as far as the eye can see.

TIPS: On a hot summer day, take a swim in either Lake Michigan or South Bar Lake, accessed from Empire's public beach — Lake Michigan Beach Park — on South Lake Michigan Drive. If you're looking for a breathtaking spot to admire Lake Michigan's natural beauty, look no further!

KICK IT UP A NOTCH: If you have the time, we suggest heading south on M-22 a few miles to Norconk Road. Head west on Norconk and park near the first corner. Look for Treat Farm Trail and follow this path all the way to Lake Michigan. Be ready to be amazed!

① **Beginner:** Little effort, kid-friendly, accessible.
② **Intermediate:** Some effort, moderate to strenuous activity.
● **Advanced:** Strenuous activity and/or some risk involved.

① **Short:** 2 hours or less.
● **Medium:** Up to 1/2 day.
③ **Long:** Full day or more; plan ahead.

○ **Wheelchair**   ● **Parking on/near site**
○ **Pets Allowed**   ○ **Kid Friendly**

Notes:

Bike

Difficulty ● ● ● ● ○
Time ● ● ● ○ ○ ○

Arcadia

Enter coordinates in phone to begin:
44.526014, -86.214493

Ride through a beautiful Michigan forest of ferns, trilliums, and fast, fun single track. Not only is Arcadia one of the best world-class mountain biking trails in northern Michigan, it's also one of the most breathtaking.

OPTIONAL SIDE TREK: After your ride, head across M-22 to the Arcadia Trailhead. Take the 2-mile hike to Lake Michigan and run down the dune for a swim in the crystal blue waters. Alternatively, head south a mile or two on M-22 and check out the view from Inspiration Point Overlook—a great place to take the family or a date.

KICK IT UP A NOTCH: In May, the Arcadia Grit & Gravel mountain bike race utilizes most of the trail for a fun, competitive experience.

TIPS: Take a friend if you can; the trail is about 10 miles long and breakdowns can happen. Carry an extra tube, a pump, and a multitool just in case. Go in spring; this trail really shines when the leaves just pop, the ferns are up, and the trilliums line the trail edges. The St Pierre parking lot is surrounded by blackberry bushes—enjoy a handful of sweet, juicy fruit!

09

① **Beginner:** Little effort, kid-friendly, accessible.
● **Intermediate:** Some effort, moderate to strenuous activity.
③ **Advanced:** Strenuous activity and/or some risk involved.

● **Short:** 2 hours or less.
② **Medium:** Up to 1/2 day.
③ **Long:** Full day or more; plan ahead.

○ **Wheelchair**   ● **Parking on/near site**
● **Pets Allowed**   ● **Kid Friendly**

Notes:

Hike

Difficulty ●●●○○○
Time ●●○○○○

Pyramid Point

Enter coordinates in phone to begin:
44.962104, -85.929960

Experience Leelanau County's most dramatic view with a twist—after the sun sinks into the horizon. A steep hike up to the bluff is worth the effort and the seclusion makes this perfect for dates or quiet relaxation. Bring a blanket and binoculars, and you've got an amazing evening ahead of you.

WHAT TO BRING: Water (especially on hot days), snacks, camera, binoculars, and a headlamp or flashlight for the hike back down in the dark. For sunsets: a blanket and a growler of wine. Please remember to take away what you bring in and we recommend not taking glass.

OPTIONAL SIDE TREK: Take the optional Pyramid Point Trail side loop to add another 1.6 miles to your hike. Approximately halfway up the trail from the parking lot, look for the side loop trail to the east. This trail weaves through beautiful forest and into some open spaces and ends at Basch Road. Stay to your right and follow the road back to the parking lot.

KICK IT UP A NOTCH: Try sand bowl jumping! Follow the sandy ridge eastward through vines and dune grass to find some of nature's perfect play areas (for adults and kids alike). Jump off the edges, roll down the banks, play a game of tag, or stand quietly to discover the unique soundproof phenomenon inside.

TIPS: Watch for poison ivy! For transporting wine in your pack, use a M22 MiiR Thermos.

● **Beginner:** Little effort, kid-friendly, accessible.
② **Intermediate:** Some effort, moderate to strenuous activity.
③ **Advanced:** Strenuous activity and/or some risk involved.

① **Short:** 2 hours or less.
● **Medium:** Up to 1/2 day.
③ **Long:** Full day or more; plan ahead.

● **Wheelchair**   ● **Parking on/near site**
● **Pets Allowed**   ● **Kid Friendly**

Notes:

Relax

Difficulty ● ○ ○ ○ ○ ○
Time ● ● ● ○ ○ ○

Frankfort Beach

Enter coordinates in phone to begin:
44.632374, -86.243613

Whether you're looking for a relaxing day in the sand or an adrenaline rush with a surfboard, there's no better place to spend a day than Frankfort Beach. Frankfort is known as one of the best surfing spots in northern Michigan. Grab your board and catch a wave when the weather's right.

WHAT TO BRING: Drinking water, a cooler with food and snacks, sunscreen, blankets/towels, swimwear, kites, sand toys, surfboards, SUPs, kayaks.

OPTIONAL SIDE TREK: Take a drive north up M-22 to check out Point Betsie Lighthouse (Microadventure no. 26), or enjoy the more secluded beach in the neighboring town of Elberta.

KICK IT UP A NOTCH: Try your hand at surfing or kiteboarding to experience what this beach is truly all about, or bike along the Betsie Valley Trail. Rent a board or bike at the Beachnut Surf Shop in Frankfort and they'll get you where you need to go!

TIPS: Hungry? Walk to the plethora of food options in Frankfort, including our local favorite, Stormcloud Brewing Company. Thirsty? Grab a growler of beer to go. The Cabbage Shed across the bay in Elberta is a popular local hangout - it's quite the experience!

● **Beginner:** Little effort, kid-friendly, accessible.
② **Intermediate:** Some effort, moderate to strenuous activity.
③ **Advanced:** Strenuous activity and/or some risk involved.

① **Short:** 2 hours or less.
② **Medium:** Up to 1/2 day.
● **Long:** Full day or more; plan ahead.

○ **Wheelchair**
○ **Pets Allowed**
● **Parking on/near site**
● **Kid Friendly**

Notes:

Sail

The Great Lakes

Difficulty ● ● ○ ○ ○ ○
Time ● ● ● ● ● ●

Enter coordinates in phone to begin:
44.757046, -85.610911

Northern Michigan is exceptional for all types of sailing, whether on smaller bodies of water or on the Big Lake. Ever wanted to try your hand at sailing? The Traverse Area Community Sailing program is a great place to start and has a wide variety of boats and lessons to choose from.

WHAT TO BRING: For any sailing adventure, you'll want to make sure you have plenty of sunscreen. Additionally, a swimsuit, water shoes, towel, water bottle, hat, and sunglasses are always a good idea. Just make sure you have a way to attach those items to your clothing or life vest in case you go overboard.

KICK IT UP A NOTCH: If you're experienced or have gone through the training programs, try your hand at one of the catamarans or Melges 24. These high-performance boats in the right wind conditions go extremely fast. If you've already mastered sailing, head out to the big lakes to experience true open water. BYOB— bring your own boat.

HISTORY: In 1994, a group of dedicated sailors wanted to share their passion for sailing with the local area youth. Traverse Area Community Sailing, a non-profit organization, now offers youth and adult sailing lessons. The program has over 70 boats from the small Sunfish to the JY 15's, lasers, catamarans, and Optimist Prams.

TIPS: If you have your own life vest, we recommend bringing it. Being comfortable out on the water is key to having a good time.

① **Beginner:** Little effort, kid-friendly, accessible.
● **Intermediate:** Some effort, moderate to strenuous activity.
③ **Advanced:** Strenuous activity and/or some risk involved.

● **Short:** 2 hours or less.
② **Medium:** Up to 1/2 day.
③ **Long:** Full day or more; plan ahead.

○ **Wheelchair**   ● **Parking on/near site**
● **Pets Allowed**   ● **Kid Friendly**

Notes:

Hike

Whaleback

Difficulty ● ● ○ ○ ○
Time ● ● ○ ○ ○ ○

Enter coordinates in phone to begin:
45.006107, -85.769901

This 10,000-year-old glacial wonder near Leland is an iconic landmark that helps to define our unique Lake Michigan coastline. Stop here to admire the 300ft fragile bluffs overlooking the Manitou Passage, first put into preservation by the Leelanau Conservancy in 1996.

WHAT TO BRING: You won't need much besides some good shoes and a camera. The one-mile trail is lined with ferns to keep you on track.

OPTIONAL SIDE TREK: Take a short drive down to Van's Beach in Leland to catch a different perspective of Whaleback while enjoying the crystal clear, sandy beach that surrounds you. On a strong north wind, grab your board to enjoy one of northern Michigan's best surfing destinations.

PROTECTING THE GREAT LAKES: M22 donates a portion of each sale to help preserve the land and water we love through the actions of the Leelanau Conservancy. Since its conception, the Leelanau Conservancy has protected more than 11,000 acres of land, including Whaleback.

TIPS: When you visit, please realize that the land on both sides of the trail is private and not open to the public. Hike this trail to claim your reward: a spectacular Lake Michigan view that brings visitors back again and again.

① **Beginner:** Little effort, kid-friendly, accessible.
● **Intermediate:** Some effort, moderate to strenuous activity.
③ **Advanced:** Strenuous activity and/or some risk involved.

① **Short:** 2 hours or less.
● **Medium:** Up to 1/2 day.
③ **Long:** Full day or more; plan ahead.

○ **Wheelchair**   ● **Parking on/near site**
○ **Pets Allowed** ● **Kid Friendly**

Notes:

Paddle

Difficulty ● ● ● ○ ○ ○
Time ● ● ● ○ ○ ○

Boardman River

Enter coordinates in phone to begin:

44.757021, -85.610710

Paddle your way down West Grand Traverse Bay's largest tributary and enjoy the unique experience of traveling right through the heart of downtown Traverse City—but this time from the water.

We suggest dropping a vehicle (or bike) at Clinch Park Marina and launching from the Hull Park boat launch on Boardman Lake. Here you can paddle around the lake then find your way to the northeast corner and begin the trip down the river. After an easy 1-2 hour paddle, you will reach West Bay. From here head west back to Clinch Park Marina.

WHAT TO BRING: A cooler for drinks, water shoes with straps (flip-flops may get lost), sunscreen, and a way to secure items like keys, phones, and wallets in case you go under (like the M22 waterproof bag).

OPTIONAL SIDE TREK: The Boardman River is known as one of the 10 best trout streams in Michigan, and is considered by many to be one of the most outstanding natural features of the Grand Traverse Bay region.

KICK IT UP A NOTCH: The Boardman River offers multiple launch locations for varied distances and paddling experiences. For a paddle geared more towards nature, put your vessel in at the Boardman Lake launch site.

TIPS: There is one dam located 1.5 miles from the mouth of the river at Union Street, but this is a short & easy portage for paddlers. If you're looking for a unique paddle experience but also enjoy a good beer every now and then, check out Kayak, Bike & Brew.

For more detailed information please visit: **kayakbikebrew.com**

● **Beginner:** Little effort, kid-friendly, accessible.
② **Intermediate:** Some effort, moderate to strenuous activity.
③ **Advanced:** Strenuous activity and/or some risk involved.

① **Short:** 2 hours or less.
② **Medium:** Up to 1/2 day.
● **Long:** Full day or more; plan ahead.

● **Wheelchair**   **●** **Parking on/near site**
● **Pets Allowed**   **●** **Kid Friendly**

Notes:

Explore

Difficulty **●**○○○○○
Time **●●●●●**○

Cherry Festival

Enter coordinates in phone to begin:
44.765841, -85.623279

From a 5k race to air shows, concerts, parades and more, the National Cherry Festival is packed full of family-friendly activities spread out over an entire week around the start of July each year.

WHAT TO BRING: Be prepared to be on your feet for a majority of your time at the Cherry Fest! Some good walking shoes and a refillable water bottle will come in very handy.

FACT: The National Cherry Festival is home to more than 150 events annually, and over 85% of these are free to the public. Traverse City area is the largest producer of tart cherries in the United States.

OPTIONAL SIDE TREK: If you are looking to take a break from the parades and crowds, Traverse City is home to many u-pick cherry orchards for the freshest experience possible. We also suggest watching the fireworks and air show from the water if possible.

TIPS: During this week in early summer, more than 500,000 visitors converge in downtown Traverse City. Parking during these times is no easy task, but the city offers a parking garage as well as street parking.

For more detailed information please visit: **downtowntc.com**

Beginner: Little effort, kid-friendly, accessible.
Intermediate: Some effort, moderate to strenuous activity.
Advanced: Strenuous activity and/or some risk involved.

Short: 2 hours or less.
Medium: Up to 1/2 day.
Long: Full day or more; plan ahead.

Wheelchair   **Parking on/near site**
Pets Allowed   **Kid Friendly**

Notes:

Drive

Pierce Stocking

Difficulty ● ○ ○ ○ ○ ○
Time ● ● ● ○ ○ ○

Enter coordinates in phone to begin:

44.852903, -86.041710

Take in some of the most astonishing scenery in the world—something you may never have thought would be possible in Michigan. Multiple stopping points along this nearly 7-mile perfectly paved stretch of road offer breathtaking views of Glen Lake, Sleeping Bear Dunes, Lake Michigan and glimpses of South Manitou Island—if you know where to look.

WHAT TO BRING: You could bring your camera to capture some of this amazing scenery and take it home with you, but a photo won't do it justice. You could always leave the camera at home in exchange for a nice picnic blanket to lay out on the sand and relax. Just make sure you have an updated park pass; these can be purchased at the gate upon arrival.

OPTIONAL SIDE TREK: The world famous Sleeping Bear Dune Climb is just minutes down the road. Bring the kids and take your turn at climbing one of Michigan's most iconic landmarks. Who can make it to the top the quickest?

KICK IT UP A NOTCH: Every fall through spring, the scenic drive is closed to all vehicle traffic due to weather. However, there are miles of trails waiting to be hiked. Bring your snowshoes in the colder months for an even more rewarding experience once you reach the iconic overlooks.

① **Beginner:** Little effort, kid-friendly, accessible.
② **Intermediate:** Some effort, moderate to strenuous activity.
● **Advanced:** Strenuous activity and/or some risk involved.

① **Short:** 2 hours or less.
② **Medium:** Up to 1/2 day.
● **Long:** Full day or more; plan ahead.

○ **Wheelchair**   ○ **Parking on/near site**
○ **Pets Allowed**   ○ **Kid Friendly**

Notes:

Surf

Difficulty ● ● ● ● ● ●
Time ● ● ● ● ● ●

The Great Lakes

Enter coordinates in phone to begin:
45.023100, -85.763216

Yes, you can surf on a lake. The Great Lakes are so large that passing storms with sustained winds pushing over hundreds of miles of water can produce ocean-like peeling waves. However, we are not going to tell you where to find all of these gems; you will have to put in the time and effort to earn that knowledge yourself.

WHAT TO BRING: Board, leash, thick wetsuit, gloves, booties, hood, wax, as well as a thermos of coffee or your favorite beverage to warm up afterward.

TOTAL ELEVATION GAIN/LOSS: 3-8 feet, depending on swell size.

WHEN TO GO: Late summer to mid-winter. Some of our best days have happened right around Christmas. Van's beach in Leland is the widely known go-to-spot in any north wind condition.

TIPS: The best spots are in the least likely of places.

JUST GETTING STARTED: If you are looking for lessons, visit Sleeping Bear Surf and Kayak in Empire or Beachnut Surf Shop in Frankfort. After you've mastered the waves, visit Loukas at Fresh Surfboards Great Lakes to get your very own custom board designed specifically for surfing the Great Lakes.

17

① **Beginner:** Little effort, kid-friendly, accessible.
② **Intermediate:** Some effort, moderate to strenuous activity.
● **Advanced:** Strenuous activity and/or some risk involved.

① **Short:** 2 hours or less.
● **Medium:** Up to 1/2 day.
③ **Long:** Full day or more; plan ahead.

○ **Wheelchair**   ● **Parking on/near site**
○ **Pets Allowed**   ○ **Kid Friendly**

Notes:

Paddle

Difficulty ● ● ● ● ● ●
Time ● ● ● ● ● ○

Enter coordinates in phone to begin:

Winter SUP

44.977215, -85.648512

You've mastered SUP over the summer, why not enjoy it year-round? If you're looking for a non-snow-based winter outdoor activity, try throwing a winter SUP adventure in the mix. Having the right gear and understanding the weather is critical to this microadventure's success.

WHAT TO BRING: Bring your SUP and a paddle, plus a leash and wearable PFD. Make sure you tell a friend where you're going and how long you'll be gone. Better yet, bring your friend along! A thick wetsuit is a must for a winter SUP session, with some warm wool socks underneath your booties. Save the fur boots and chunky winter clothes for a photo shoot; they are a potential hazard out on the water, especially if you fall in.

OPTIONAL SIDE TREK: Try paddling non-accessible shorelines for views that you can't get anywhere but from the water.

KICK IT UP A NOTCH: Any water activity in the winter can be dangerous, so this microadventure is already kicked up a notch.

TIPS: Always paddle upwind first, stay close to shore, and check the weather before you head out to make sure the wind is not forecasted to increase. Pick up a M22 Thermos for one of your favorite post-winter activities.

18

① **Beginner:** Little effort, kid-friendly, accessible.
② **Intermediate:** Some effort, moderate to strenuous activity.
● **Advanced:** Strenuous activity and/or some risk involved.

① **Short:** 2 hours or less.
● **Medium:** Up to 1/2 day.
③ **Long:** Full day or more; plan ahead.

○ **Wheelchair**   ● **Parking on/near site**
○ **Pets Allowed**   ● **Kid Friendly**

Notes:

Conquer

The M22 Challenge

Difficulty ●●●●●
Time ●●●○○

Enter coordinates in phone to begin:
44.885203, -86.035782

Experience the venue of "the most beautiful race in America." This run/bike/paddle course takes you up the Sleeping Bear Dunes, around the picturesque Glen Lakes, and out into the crystal clear waters of Little Glen Lake. This will surely be one of your new favorite courses!

WHAT TO BRING: Running shoes, road bike, kayak or SUP, and determination. If you don't own a kayak for the water portion, they can be rented for the day from Crystal River Outfitters.

OPTIONAL SIDE TREK: One of our favorite camping spots, D.H. Day Campground, is just around the corner. This campground is one of the best places in the area to unwind after a good day's exercise.

COURSE INFO: The race starts off with a 2.5-mile run that includes a grueling climb up the Dune Climb. Don't worry, the view from the top makes it worth it. Next, the 17-mile road course circles both Glen Lakes and leads up Inspiration Point—the 446ft climb everyone fears. After the descent, it's a quick 4 miles back to the transition area. From Little Glen Picnic Area, the 2.5-mile paddle course heads straight out along the west shore of Little Glen lake for about a mile, then cuts directly across the lake where you follow the northern shoreline back to the park.

TIPS: Visit **M22challenge.com** for course maps, dates, registration information, or even to volunteer at the next M22 Challenge. The event is always held on the second Saturday in June.

① **Beginner:** Little effort, kid-friendly, accessible.
② **Intermediate:** Some effort, moderate to strenuous activity.
● **Advanced:** Strenuous activity and/or some risk involved.

① **Short:** 2 hours or less.
② **Medium:** Up to 1/2 day.
● **Long:** Full day or more; plan ahead.

○ **Wheelchair**
○ **Pets Allowed**
● **Parking on/near site**
● **Kid Friendly**

Notes:

Backpack

North Manitou

Difficulty ● ● ● ● ○
Time ● ● ● ● ●

Enter coordinates in phone to begin:

45.121740, -85.977056

Whether you're looking to turn back time, or just escape from the hectic world for a few days, there is no better place in northern Michigan to experience the simpler aspects of life and enjoy the solitude that North Manitou Island offers on this pack-in pack-out journey.

WHAT TO BRING: Bring a trusty old watch. If you venture to the west side of the island, your phone will pick up the central time zone—one hour behind most of Michigan. This could lead to confusion or problems with timing on your way back since you will need to make it back to the ferry dock by a certain hour on your day of departure. Additionally, bring everything you will need to survive out of your backpack. An extra day's worth of food is recommended as well.

BEFORE YOU LEAVE: Ferry tickets to the island should be purchased as far in advance as possible to ensure you get a spot on the boat. You will also need to have a Sleeping Bear Dunes National Lakeshore park pass, which can be purchased on site in Leland.

KICK IT DOWN A NOTCH: You can forgo the backcountry camping permits and instead stay at one of North Manitou Island's designated Village Campground Campsites. Either way, camping permits will need to be purchased before you depart at the Manitou Island Transit ticket office.

TIPS: There is only one restroom on the whole island, so don't forget TP or a shovel to bury it! Please leave no trace of your visit; this island is all of ours to enjoy. Beware of ticks.

● **Beginner:** Little effort, kid-friendly, accessible.
② **Intermediate:** Some effort, moderate to strenuous activity.
③ **Advanced:** Strenuous activity and/or some risk involved.

● **Short:** 2 hours or less.
② **Medium:** Up to 1/2 day.
③ **Long:** Full day or more; plan ahead.

● **Wheelchair**   ● **Parking on/near site**
● **Pets Allowed**   ○ **Kid Friendly**

Notes:

Sip

M22 Wine

Difficulty ● ○ ○ ○ ○ ○
Time ● ● ○ ○ ○ ○

Enter coordinates in phone to begin:

44.897888, -85.984784

Experience the wine bar inside the M22 Glen Arbor store, or the outdoor wine patio for a true taste of northern Michigan. M22 has partnered with the renowned winemakers at Black Star Farms to custom blend 16 specialty wines for M22.

WHAT TO BRING: $6 will get you 5 pours of wine and a souvenir M22 small stemless tasting glass. Don't forget your ID!

OPTIONAL SIDE TREK: Grab a bottle of wine, an M22 corkscrew and head down to the boat launch at the end of Lake Street in Glen Arbor to enjoy the bottle and a sunset. M22 in Glen Arbor is open until 9 pm in July & August, and you know what time the sun sets in the summer!

KICK IT UP A NOTCH: For $3 more you can sample all three of our M22 Premium Wines- Bubbly Brut, the Crystal River Bubbly and the Vintner's Red. Enjoyed what you tasted? Buy four bottles of any wine to get 10% off.

FACT: Taste the Crystal River Bubbly, a sweet champagne style wine named after the Crystal River across the street. The Crystal runs almost entirely through Sleeping Bear Dunes National Lakeshore. Check out the Crystal River Microadventure (no. 02) for more information.

TIPS: Get ready to sip and shop. The wine bar is surrounded by the entire M22 product line.

21

● **Beginner:** Little effort, kid-friendly, accessible.
② **Intermediate:** Some effort, moderate to strenuous activity.
③ **Advanced:** Strenuous activity and/or some risk involved.

① **Short:** 2 hours or less.
② **Medium:** Up to 1/2 day.
● **Long:** Full day or more; plan ahead.

● **Wheelchair**   ● **Parking on/near site**
● **Pets Allowed**   ● **Kid Friendly**

Notes:

Experience

White Birch Lodge

Difficulty ● ○ ○ ○ ○ ○
Time ● ● ● ● ● ○

Enter coordinates in phone to begin:

44.886381, -85.399732

Nestled at the end of Meguzee Point peninsula on Elk Lake, White Birch Lodge is one of the few remaining family-focused, all-inclusive resorts in northern Michigan. Family-owned and operated since 1958, White Birch Lodge features an incredible water sports program, which includes waterskiing, wakeboarding, and more; all in a private, safe lakefront setting.

OPTIONAL SIDE TREK: If you don't feel like water skiing, White Birch Lodge also features endless activities including basketball, tennis, soccer, shuffleboard, ping-pong, kayaking, golf and more. Alternatively, head to downtown Elk Rapids to escape the hustle and bustle of downtown Traverse City in the summer while still experiencing some of the best activities that any northern Michigan town has to offer.

KICK IT UP A NOTCH: White Birch Lodge offers Michigan's most extensive water sports program. From the thrill of water skiing, wakeboarding, and tubing behind their fleet of MasterCrafts, to the quiet exhilaration of kayaking, sailing, or SUP; White Birch Lodge offers it all. Their enthusiastic staff will be in the water with you every step of the way with all the assistance and instruction you need to go from beginner to advanced. There is a ski show put on weekly by their staff and is sure to entertain everyone on Thursday evenings mid-June to mid-August.

For more detailed information visit: **whitebirchlodge.org**

22

● **Beginner:** Little effort, kid-friendly, accessible.
② **Intermediate:** Some effort, moderate to strenuous activity.
③ **Advanced:** Strenuous activity and/or some risk involved.

① **Short:** 2 hours or less.
● **Medium:** Up to 1/2 day.
③ **Long:** Full day or more; plan ahead.

● **Wheelchair**   ● **Parking on/near site**
● **Pets Allowed**   ● **Kid Friendly**

Notes:

Bike

Difficulty ● ● ○ ○ ○ ○
Time ● ● ● ● ○ ○

Heritage Trail

Enter coordinates in phone to begin:
44.897994, -85.984268

The Sleeping Bear Heritage Trail is a paved, non-motorized trail that runs throughout many areas of Sleeping Bear Dunes National Lakeshore. The trail is currently 22.5 miles running from Empire to Port Oneida. Pick up the trail at many points- Glen Arbor, Empire, Port Oneida, or DH Day Campground.

WHAT TO BRING: Meet at The Cyclery in downtown Glen Arbor for bike rentals. The staff will set you up with a hybrid bike, which is perfect for handling the terrain (mostly pavement) of the SBHT. They also offer kids bikes, Burleys, Weehoos and Trail-a-Bikes so everyone can enjoy the trail.

OPTIONAL SIDE TREK: Stop by M22 Glen Arbor for wine tasting at the end of your day's adventure. Enjoy some of the 15 custom blends offered by M22. Sample 5 wines for $6 and keep your M22 small stemless glass. The Hard Cider will definitely quench your thirst after biking!

KICK IT UP A NOTCH: Bike the trail south towards Glen Haven. Here you can hike the Sleeping Bear Point Trail right through the heart of the dunes. You'll catch some amazing glimpses of Lake Michigan and the Manitou Islands.

TIPS: A National Park Pass is recommended when biking the Sleeping Bear Heritage Trail, as the trail goes almost entirely through Sleeping Bear Dunes. The Cyclery & M22 Glen Arbor sell both weekly and annual park passes.

● **Beginner:** Little effort, kid-friendly, accessible.
② **Intermediate:** Some effort, moderate to strenuous activity.
③ **Advanced:** Strenuous activity and/or some risk involved.

● **Short:** 2 hours or less.
② **Medium:** Up to 1/2 day.
③ **Long:** Full day or more; plan ahead.

○ **Wheelchair**   ● **Parking on/near site**
○ **Pets Allowed**   ● **Kid Friendly**

Notes:

Soar

Traverse City

Difficulty ● ○ ○ ○ ○ ○
Time ● ● ○ ○ ○ ○

Enter coordinates in phone to begin:

44.745427, -85.583219

Experience the adventure of a lifetime and take in the sights of the most beautiful place in America like never before - from above. While riding shotgun with some of the most experienced pilots in the area, even those that have lived here their entire lives will be blown away by this experience.

BEFORE YOU FLY: Up to 3 passengers per flight (with a 2 rider minimum on most tours- weight restrictions may apply- call for details) all helicopter tour packages are fully refundable or may be rescheduled no questions asked! All tours cancelled due to weather can be rescheduled or refunded at customer request.

KICK IT UP A NOTCH: Flying in a helicopter is an interactive experience and entirely different than flying in a plane. Our favorite part of this adventure is the music the pilots coordinate with the flight path. Everyone wears headphones that are connected together, and the pilots have synced a roller coaster type flight route with amazing theatrical music. It's something you must experience first-hand!

ABOUT THE PILOTS: Michael Terfehr, the President of TC Helicopter Tours, first flew solo on his 16th birthday, and received his pilot's license on his 17th birthday. Currently, Michael has over 10,000 flight hours in many types of aircraft, including a Piper Cub, Bell 407, Cessna 185 Float Plane, Gulfstream IV, and a L-39 Fighter Jet.

Kurtis Dellicker has over 1,100 flight hours and throughout his career, has served in the US Army (retired), Monongalia Emergency Medical Services, North Flight EMS, TC Helicopters and 45 North Aviation.

When you book your flight make sure you let them know the M22 crew sent you!

For more detailed information please visit: **tchelicoptertours.com**

① **Beginner:** Little effort, kid-friendly, accessible.
② **Intermediate:** Some effort, moderate to strenuous activity.
● **Advanced:** Strenuous activity and/or some risk involved.

① **Short:** 2 hours or less.
● **Medium:** Up to 1/2 day.
③ **Long:** Full day or more; plan ahead.

○ **Wheelchair**   ● **Parking on/near site**
○ **Pets Allowed**   ○ **Kid Friendly**

Notes:

Ride

Difficulty ● ● ● ● ● ●
Time ● ● ● ● ○ ○

Pierce Stocking

Enter coordinates in phone to begin:
44.853124, -86.040783

For one of the most challenging and beautiful road bike routes in northern Michigan, look no further than the familiar Pierce Stocking Scenic Drive. Known around the world as one of the most scenic locations in America, this loop takes both cars and bikes along a perfectly paved stretch of road, offering multiple stopping points along the way.

WHAT TO BRING: Bring a bike with a proper rear cassette! You'll want to have gearing that can handle both the sweeping downhills and grueling climbs that Pierce Stocking will throw at you. Make sure you have an updated park pass upon arrival. Passes can be purchased at the booth upon arrival.

KICK IT UP A NOTCH: After you've become familiar with the course, why stop at just one lap? One of our favorite workouts is a three-lap tour of Pierce Stocking, stopping at our favorite overlook, #9, on the final loop. Three laps end up coming out at just under 20 miles, but with almost 2,000ft of elevation gain.

FACT: As beautiful as it may be, this is not an easy or lighthearted course. We suggest riding one or two laps at a more casual pace to get familiar with the ascents and descents before setting your sights on the KOMs (Strava's King of the Mountain). As with any road ride, be aware and courteous of those approaching from behind in their vehicles.

① **Beginner:** Little effort, kid-friendly, accessible.
● **Intermediate:** Some effort, moderate to strenuous activity.
③ **Advanced:** Strenuous activity and/or some risk involved.

● **Short:** 2 hours or less.
② **Medium:** Up to 1/2 day.
③ **Long:** Full day or more; plan ahead.

○ **Wheelchair**   ● **Parking on/near site**
○ **Pets Allowed**   ○ **Kid Friendly**

Notes:

Paddle

Difficulty ● ● ● ○ ○ ○
Time ● ● ○ ○ ○ ○

Women's SUP Night

Enter coordinates in phone to begin:

44.900647, -85.955504

Women's SUP Nights are a great way to combine a social night with fitness all while appreciating the beauty of northern Michigan from the water. Each week, locations change, allowing paddlers to view as much of northern Michigan as possible from a unique perspective: stand up paddling.

WHAT TO EXPECT: You will meet new friends, challenge yourself, and leave the night knowing you did something good for your body. Women's SUP Nights take place every Thursday (since 2011) in the summer. Visit: **facebook.com/womenssup**

HOW TO GET THERE: The location changes every week, but most paddles are based out of the Traverse City area. Locations can be found on the Facebook page. Several events are "destination paddles" based out of Glen Arbor, Frankfort, and Leland. After the events, join the girls for dinner on the beach or at a local eatery. Any cancellations due to weather are posted by 3pm the day of the paddle.

GETTING STARTED: All events are free and SUP at your own risk. Bring your own SUP, paddle, safety gear, and positive attitude. Unless it's a special event, Women's SUP Nights are not open to your dude friends, children, or pets. It's "girls' night out!" To get the most out of the night, you should be able to paddle standing up for 1.5hrs. Experience levels vary and typical paddles bring in 20-30 paddlers, so you are likely to find someone of similar ability in the group. No one is left behind, and it is asked that no one turns back early. Be prepared for occasional choppy water and some upwind paddling.

Beginner: Little effort, kid-friendly, accessible.
② **Intermediate:** Some effort, moderate to strenuous activity.
③ **Advanced:** Strenuous activity and/or some risk involved.

① **Short:** 2 hours or less.
● **Medium:** Up to 1/2 day.
③ **Long:** Full day or more; plan ahead.

● **Wheelchair**   ● **Parking on/near site**
● **Pets Allowed**   ● **Kid Friendly**

Notes:

Drive

Lighthouse Tour

Difficulty ● ○ ○ ○ ○ ○
Time ● ● ● ○ ○ ○

Enter coordinates in phone to begin:
44.633602, -86.244909

In a state with more lighthouses than any other in the country, you don't have to travel far to experience some of these great beacons. Built during the golden age of Great Lakes passage—one of the most traveled waterways in the world—these lighthouses have kept travelers safe since the late 1800's.

WHERE TO START: If you want to make a day trip out of it and experience four of our favorites, begin your nearly 70-mile trip in the quiet town of Frankfort. Here, you'll find the Frankfort North Breakwater Lighthouse, nestled at the end of the north pier. The remainder of our recommended tour will take you up past the northernmost point on M-22 in Northport, with stops at Point Betsie light, Manning Memorial Light in Empire, and Grand Traverse Lighthouse in Northport.

WHEN TO GO: Voted "Best Scenic Autumn Drive" by both USA Today and 10Best readers, there is no better time to drive M-22 than in the fall. When the leaves begin to turn - usually around the second or third week in October - the drive between each lighthouse will be even more spectacular.

OPTIONAL SIDE TREK: In between lighthouses, stop at some of our favorite restaurants along the way to grab a bite to eat. Our selections include Empire Village Inn, Art's Tavern in Glen Arbor, the Cheese Shop in Fishtown followed by ice cream at Harbor House, or the Garage Bar & Grill in Northport. Hoping to see a freighter pass by during your stop at one of the lighthouses? Visit **marinetraffic.com** to see a live update of their locations on the Great Lakes.

 Refer to map at front of book for lighthouse locations.

① **Beginner:** Little effort, kid-friendly, accessible.
● **Intermediate:** Some effort, moderate to strenuous activity.
③ **Advanced:** Strenuous activity and/or some risk involved.

① **Short:** 2 hours or less.
② **Medium:** Up to 1/2 day.
● **Long:** Full day or more; plan ahead.

○ **Wheelchair** ○ **Parking on/near site**
● **Pets Allowed** ● **Kid Friendly**

Notes:

Camp

Difficulty ● ● ● ○ ○
Time ● ● ● ● ● ○

Power Island

Enter coordinates in phone to begin:
44.864444, -85.571160

Power Island is a 200-acre nature preserve with a history almost as diverse as the island itself. For almost half a century in the 1900s, this piece of land took on the name Ford Island, after its then-owner Henry Ford. The beauty of the island has long been known by those willing to get there, making for one of the best camping locations in the Midwest.

HOW TO GET THERE: From Clinch Park in downtown Traverse City, it's about a 6.5-mile journey out to the island. Instead of leaving from town here, we recommend launching in a canoe filled with your gear from Bower's Harbor Marina, as the journey is then cut down by over 3 miles each way. Be sure to monitor the weather, as crossing the open water can be a tricky and dangerous task from a canoe. Currently, there is no ferry service available.

BEFORE YOU GO: There are ten accommodating campsites on the island, each one with its own picnic table, cooking grill and campfire circle. There are restroom services on the island, but no trash dump. Please bring a bag to pack out any and all trash that you may bring in. Before your stay, make sure to book one of the first-come, first-serve campsites at **grandtraverse.org**

ONCE YOU'RE THERE: The island is home to more than 5 miles of trails for you to hike or run. If you're searching for hills, take the North Ridge Trail up to Eagle's Nest lookout for the best view on the island. Alternatively, bring your snorkeling gear to explore the drop-off on the east side of the island, followed by a nice evening cookout back at your campsite with friends.

● **Beginner:** Little effort, kid-friendly, accessible.
② **Intermediate:** Some effort, moderate to strenuous activity.
③ **Advanced:** Strenuous activity and/or some risk involved.

① **Short:** 2 hours or less.
● **Medium:** Up to 1/2 day.
③ **Long:** Full day or more; plan ahead.

○ **Wheelchair**   ○ **Parking on/near site**
○ **Pets Allowed**   ● **Kid Friendly**

Notes:

Relax

Difficulty ● ● ○ ○ ○
Time ● ● ● ○ ○

North Bar

Enter coordinates in phone to begin:
44.843795, -86.061030

In a place with more coastline than any other state in the country besides Alaska, Michigan certainly has its fair share of wonderful beaches. North Bar Lake offers everything that one could possibly imagine, truly rivaling some of the best beaches in the world.

This small spring-fed lake measures about 900 feet across and 100 feet deep, with a one-foot-deep sandy channel that connects to Lake Michigan — it's the ultimate place for kids (and grownups) to explore and play.

WHAT TO BRING: Bring a SUP and paddle the warm, calm waters of North Bar Lake before heading right out into Lake Michigan to cool off. Feel like having a pizza party on the beach? One of our favorite pizza joints - Empire Village Inn - is just down the road. In addition, the small creek connecting North Bar to Lake Michigan can be perfect for skimboarding.

OPTIONAL SIDE TREK: One of the most scenic drives in the world, Pierce Stocking, is just a few miles away. Take in all of the sights along the 6-mile, winding drive before heading down to relax on the beach. Be sure to stop at the often forgotten overlook #11 - you'll be glad you did.

TIPS: Recent water levels are historically high in the Great Lakes, making most of the beaches in the region smaller than normal. As space on the sand is minimized, it can be tempting to climb the small dunes around the North Bar area. To help preserve this beautiful place, please keep off the dunes wherever preservation signs are present.

29

① **Beginner:** Little effort, kid-friendly, accessible.
② **Intermediate:** Some effort, moderate to strenuous activity.
● **Advanced:** Strenuous activity and/or some risk involved.

① **Short:** 2 hours or less.
● **Medium:** Up to 1/2 day.
③ **Long:** Full day or more; plan ahead.

○ **Wheelchair**   ● **Parking on/near site**
○ **Pets Allowed**   ○ **Kid Friendly**

Notes:

Kiteboard

Wind & Waves

Difficulty ● ● ● ● ●
Time ● ● ● ● ○

Enter coordinates in phone to begin:
44.846529, -85.447233

Back in 2002, the founders of M22, Matt and Keegan Myers, opened the first kiteboarding school in the Midwest. For over 10 years, the brothers taught kiteboarding around the world and worked as editors of Kiteboarding Magazine. After traveling the globe, the brothers landed right back home where it all began: northern Michigan.

WHAT TO BRING: Most days in Michigan, a 12M or 16M kite is the best call. We use the app Windfinder for local forecasts as it's the most accurate. Maple Bay and Platte River Point offer both flatwater and choppy conditions, so bring your twin tip. Frankfort and Leland are best for waves, so be sure to bring your surfboard and possibly an 8M kite.

TIPS: The best kiting spot close to Traverse City is Maple Bay, just a few miles south of Elk Rapids. This area is owned by the Grand Traverse Regional Land Conservancy and is open to the public.

This is the best spot for learning as there are miles of shallow, sandy bottom lake with beautiful desolate beaches. Vans Beach in Leland is best on a strong north wind and produces amazing right breaking waves. Frankfort works great on a south or south-west wind just on the north side of the pier. If the wind blows west, head to Platte River Point for super fun shore break and a beautiful river that dumps right into Lake Michigan.

Please respect our special kiteboarding locations, ensure the safety of pedestrians on the beach, and take everything with you that you bring.

Visit **mackiteboarding.com** in Grand Haven for lessons and gear.

● **Beginner:** Little effort, kid-friendly, accessible.
② **Intermediate:** Some effort, moderate to strenuous activity.
③ **Advanced:** Strenuous activity and/or some risk involved.

① **Short:** 2 hours or less.
● **Medium:** Up to 1/2 day.
③ **Long:** Full day or more; plan ahead.

● **Wheelchair**
● **Pets Allowed**
● **Parking on/near site**
● **Kid Friendly**

Notes:

Roadtrip

M-22

Difficulty ● ○ ○ ○ ○ ○
Time ● ● ● ○ ○

Enter coordinates in phone to begin:

44.769042, -85.634260

Come see for yourself why M-22 is considered one of the most beautiful drives in the entire country. M-22 was voted "America's Favorite Scenic Autumn Drive" by both USA Today and 10Best readers. Stretching 116 miles from Traverse City to Manistee, our favorite highway will take you along the shores of Lake Michigan.

WHERE TO START: If you're feeling adventurous, why not spend the day taking in all that M-22 has to offer; from start to finish. Heading east out of Traverse City, M-22 will bring you up and around the Leelanau Peninsula before heading south on your way to Manistee - a quiet coastal town full of charm and access to beautiful Lake Michigan.

OPTIONAL SIDE TREK: There are many worthwhile detours from M-22 itself that can provide some of the most unforgettable, secluded scenery in the region. If you have some extra time along your drive, bring a map along and see where some of these coastal roads may lead you. This is how we've found some of our best kiteboarding spots throughout the years, and you never know what you could discover at the end of the next dirt road. Adventure starts here!

OUR FAVORITE STOPS: There is no shortage of places to stop and eat along this iconic route. Some of our favorites include The Cheese Shop in Fishtown, Leland, Art's Tavern in Glen Arbor, Stormcloud Brewing in Frankfort, and Iron Works Cafe in Manistee - a local nonprofit that supports regional farmers and provides access to healthy meals for nearby residents. If you're looking to stretch your legs a bit after all of that time in the car, look no further than the famous Sleeping Bear Dunes or the Arcadia Roadside Lookout.

The Road
Less Traveled.

Growing up in a cabin in the woods, miles from town and without any other neighbors, we learned early on the value of our environment and the importance of being immersed in nature. This thirst for adventure led us into the world of kiteboarding for many years.

Kiteboarding took us around the world searching out the best wind and waves we could find. Ultimately, we were led right back home to where it all began: northern Michigan and the Great Lakes. We loved northern Michigan from the beginning and realized there is no other place like it. With miles of freshwater sandy bottom lakes, remote beaches, and lush forests, this is the kiting worlds best-kept secret.

Today, we still kite as much as possible but also fill our free time showing our children the potential for adventure right out our door. They are growing up in the same woods we did, miles from town, playing in nature. That same childhood curiosity for adventure has encouraged us to share these simple experiences with you.

We hope you've enjoyed the information gathered in this book and are inspired to get up, get out, and experience a microadventure for yourself.

Matt + Kaegan